Junior
How to Draw
Cars, Trucks and Planes

P9-APF-844

Published by Top That! Publishing plc
Tide Mill Way, Woodbridge, Suffolk, IP12 1AP, UK
www.topthatpublishing.com
Copyright © 2013 Top That! Publishing plc
All rights reserved.
0 2 4 6 8 9 7 5 3 1
Printed and bound in China

Introduction

Have you always wanted to draw cars, trucks and planes, but were put off because they looked too difficult? Have no fear! This book shows you a fun and easy way to draw vehicles!

Just follow the tips and step-by-step instructions, and you'll soon learn a set of basic drawing techniques that you can then apply to any subject.

Top Tip!

To draw good, clean lines, you need to keep your pencils nice and sharp with a pencil sharpener.

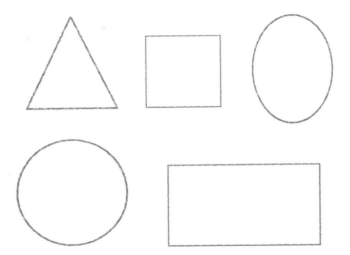

Basic Shapes

When you want to draw an object, a good way to start is to look at the object carefully and to break it down in your mind into a series of simple shapes—triangles, squares, rectangles, circles and ovals.

Notice which shapes are bigger or smaller than others, and where they join together. Look carefully at their angles and proportions. Spend time just looking before you pick up your pencil!

Tools of the Trade

You will need a pencil, an eraser, a pencil sharpener, a ruler, a fine black marker pen and fiber-tip pens or pencils for coloring in your drawings.

Four Simple Steps

You can apply the "basic shapes" technique to drawing any subject, including cars, trucks and planes. You can use it for simple front-on and side-on views, as well as for more complicated angled views. All it takes is four simple steps...

Top Tip!

Sketch your pencil guidelines lightly, otherwise, when you come to erase them, you will see traces of them on the finished drawing.

Construction lines

Step 1. First, break the vehicle down into basic shapes. Sketch them in pencil.

Step 2. Next, sketch construction lines to help you get the right angles, and draw a pencil outline.

Step 3. Build up the detail, then go over your pencil outline in pen.

Step 4. Erase the guidelines and add color to bring your picture to life.

Perspective

Many of the drawings in this book show objects seen from an angle. When you look at a drawing, it should be obvious where the artist was in relation to what they were drawing. This is known as "perspective."

The basic rule of perspective is that objects in the distance appear smaller than those closer to the viewer.

3

Car Side-on

Use these simple shapes to help you draw the side-on view of a car.

Step 1. First, with a pencil and ruler, lightly sketch a line for the road. Next, draw a long rectangle. Add two circles for wheels and a smaller rectangle on top of the first one, positioned just off-center.

Step 2. Next, sketch construction lines to show the angles of the car. Draw them for the top and sides of the windows, the main body angles, and a vertical line where the doors meet.

Step 3. Now draw the outline of the car's body. Notice that the hood and trunk slope downward. Draw the window shapes, the wheel arches and two smaller circles inside the wheels.

Step 4. Go over your outline with a fine black marker pen. You can now erase the pencil guidelines and start to draw in the finer details. Draw the lights, wing mirror, door handles and windshield.

Step 5. Erase any remaining pencil guidelines and color in your car with fiber-tip pens or pencils.

Car Front-on

Now that you've mastered a car from the side, see if you can tackle one from the front!

Step 1. Sketch two small squares for wheels and two rectangles for the body.

Step 2. Sketch a center line and construction lines for the angles. Then draw the car's outline.

Step 3. Go over the outline in black pen and add detail—radiator, lights, mirrors.

Step 4. Erase the pencil guidelines and finish your drawing by coloring it in.

Creating Different-shaped Cars

Use these basic shapes to create a small car, a sports car and a station wagon. Look carefully to see how the shape and angles of each car are different.

Small Car

1 **Step 1.** For this car, draw the smaller rectangle right of center.

2 **Step 2.** Add construction lines to give you the angles of the body. Then draw the outline.

3 **Step 3.** Go over the outline in pen, add details and color in.

Sports Car

1 **Step 1.** For a sports car, the two rectangles are centered.

2 **Step 2.** Using construction lines, sketch the short roof, curved hood and slanting tail end.

3 **Step 3.** Outline in pen, add details and color in brightly.

Station Wagon

1 **Step 1.** For the station wagon, line up the rectangles to the right.

2 **Step 2.** Add construction lines to give you the angles of the sloping windshield and hood.

3 **Step 3.** Go over your outline in pen, add details and color in.

Other Cars to Try

Every car looks different. See if you can sketch these well-known cars using the techniques you have learned.

Top Tip!

Sketching construction lines will help you to get the angles of the bodywork right. Lightly sketch them in pencil every time you draw a car!

Beetle Front-on

1

Step 1. Sketch these basic shapes. The middle rectangle is slightly taller than the top one.

2

Step 2. Next, sketch in construction lines to give you the angles, then draw the outline.

3

Step 3. Add details and go over your outline in black pen.

4

Step 4. Erase the guidelines and color in your Beetle.

Beetle Side-on

1

Step 1. Sketch the basic shapes for a side-on view of a car, plus a line for the road. Notice that the top rectangle is not quite central.

3

Step 2. Next, sketch construction lines and the car's curved outline. Add windows and wheels.

4

Step 3. Add further details, then go over your pencil outline in black pen.

Step 4. Erase the pencil guidelines and choose a nice bright color for your Beetle.

Mini Cooper Front-on

1

Step 1. First, sketch two small rectangles for wheels, then a large rectangle with a smaller one on top.

2

Step 2. Next, sketch construction lines to give you the angles of the car's body. Draw the outline, adding headlights and wing mirrors.

3

Step 3. Add the wide radiator, license plate and other details. Then go over your outline in pen.

4

Step 4. Erase the pencil guidelines and color in your car.

Wrangler Jeep Front-on

Step 1. Start with a line for the road. Then sketch two squares, wide apart, for wheels, topped by two rectangles.

Step 2. Next, build up the outline using construction lines to give you the angles.

Step 3. Add details and go over your outline in black pen.

Step 4. Erase the pencil guidelines and color in your jeep.

Chevy Bel Air Front-on

Step 1. First, sketch the basic shapes—two small squares for wheels, then a wide rectangle with a smaller one on top, positioned centrally.

Step 3. Add further details, then go over your outline in black pen.

Fact File

The Chevrolet Bel Air, with its hooded headlights and stylish tail fins, was a classic car of the 1950s. It has appeared in many movies.

Step 2. Next, sketch construction lines to give you the angles for the body, which curves in and out. Draw the outline.

Step 4. Erase the pencil guidelines and color in your classic Chevy Bel Air.

Wrangler Jeep Side-on

Step 1. Sketch a line for the road, two circles for wheels and a large rectangle, to the right of center. Add a smaller rectangle on top, also to the right of center.

Step 2. Next, build up the outline, giving a slight slant to the jeep's roof, hood and tail end.

Step 3. Add details such as hubcaps (wheel covers). Then go over your outline in black pen.

Step 4. Erase any pencil guidelines and color in your jeep.

Try These Cars

The Porsche 911, the Pagani Zonda and the powerful F1 racing car are all built for speed, but are very different shapes.

Top Tip!

Continue to use construction lines in all your vehicle drawings. They'll help you to get the bodywork and windows looking right.

Pagani Zonda

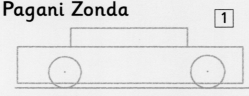

Step 1. Sketch a line for the road, two circles, a large rectangle close to the road and a small rectangle centered on top.

Step 2. Draw the car's outline. The body sweeps down under the window and curves up at the back, out of the box.

Step 3. Add details, including the triangular spoiler at the back that helps the car to grip the road. Go over your outline in black pen.

Step 4. Erase any pencil lines and color in your speedy supercar.

Porsche 911

Step 1. Sketch a line for the road and two circles for wheels. Next add a long rectangle centered over the wheels. Then draw a small rectangle on top, to the right of center.

Step 2. Draw the car's curved outline, with its long, sloping back. Add windows and wheels.

Step 3. Add the details shown here, and then go over your pencil sketch in black pen.

Step 4. Erase the pencil guidelines and color your Porsche in a bright, bold color.

F1 Racing Car

Step 1. Sketch a road line and two circles for wheels. Next, draw a long rectangle very close to the road line, far to the right of center. Add a thin rectangle on top and an almost square rectangle at the tail end.

Step 2. Study the outline shape of the racing car and copy it into your guideline boxes.

Step 3. Add more detail. Then go over your pencil sketch in pen.

Step 4. Erase the guidelines and decorate your amazing F1.

Stylish Sports Cars

Time to test out your drawing skills on these three fun, super-cool sports cars. Ready? Get set, go!

Fact File

Ferruccio Lamborghini, from Italy, started out building tractors. He went on to design stylish supercars made for long-distance travel.

Bugatti Veyron

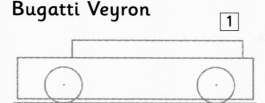

Step 1. Sketch the guideline shapes for the Bugatti Veyron. The large rectangle is slightly to the left of center, and the small one is to the right.

Step 2. Next, sketch the car's curved outline and add some details.

Step 3. Build up the detail, especially on the wheels. Then go over your outline in black pen.

Step 4. Erase the guidelines and choose a smart color for this very stylish car.

Lamborghini Gallardo

Step 1. Sketch a line for the road, two circles for wheels and a long rectangle slightly to the left of center. Add a small rectangle on top, almost lining up with the right edge of the large rectangle.

Step 2. Next, sketch the sleek outline shape of the car with its short, curved hood.

Step 3. Add the details shown here, and then go over your pencil outline in black pen.

Step 4. Erase the pencil guidelines and color in your speedy, comfortable supercar.

Morgan Aero

Step 2. Next, draw the car's outline and the sleek curve of the bodywork over the front wheel.

Step 1. Sketch a line for the road, two circles and a large rectangle slightly to the left of center—make the right edge of the rectangle slightly shorter than the left edge. Add a long, thin rectangle on top.

Step 3. Add detail, then go over your outline in black pen.

Step 4. Erase the pencil guidelines and color in your classic sports car.

Car at an Angle

Here is the basic technique for drawing a car at an angle. Add your own construction lines to help you with the angles.

Fact File

The first car race took place in Paris in 1894. Since then motor racing has become one of the most popular sports in the world.

1

Step 1. Start by sketching a large, slanting rectangle (called a parallelogram). Then sketch another, smaller one on top.

2

Step 2. Next, draw two more boxes exactly the same as the first two, but slightly lower down and to the right.

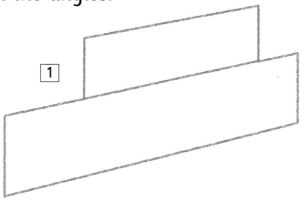

3

Step 3. To make your boxes look three-dimensional, join up the top and bottom of the two small boxes with four slanting lines, and the top and bottom of the two large boxes with another four slanting lines.

4

Step 4. Now your car is starting to take shape! Carefully erase some of the pencil lines, as shown, and add the outlines of the wheels.

Step 5. Next, draw the "side" of the car, fitting it into the guideline boxes, as shown.

5

Step 6. Continue to build up the car's body, adding in the front and roof. Use a ruler to help you keep both ends of each line an equal distance from the box edges.

6

7

Step 7. Once you are happy with the outline, erase the ends of the pencil lines that you drew to get the angles right.

8

Step 8. Go over your sketch in black pen and add details such as doors, lights, radiator and bumpers.

9

Step 9. Finally, erase any remaining pencil guidelines and color in your drawing using pens or pencils.

Dumper Truck

Have fun drawing this mighty dumper truck.

Side-on View

Step 1. Using a pencil and ruler, sketch a road line, two circles and two rectangles, as above.

Step 2. Using the boxes as a position guide, sketch in the outline of the truck.

Step 3. Build up the details, then go over the pencil lines in black pen.

Step 4. Erase the guidelines and complete your dumper truck by coloring it in.

Front-on View

Step 1. First, sketch two small squares and two large rectangles.

Step 2. Next, sketch the truck's outline into your guideline boxes.

Step 3. Add lights and other details, and go over the sketch in pen.

Step 4. Complete your mighty truck by coloring it in!

Angled View

Step 1. Sketch the shapes above to create guideline boxes for an angled view of the truck.

Step 2. Next, sketch the outline of the truck inside the boxes. Use the boxes as a guide to make sure your lines and angles are correct.

Step 3. Add further detail to your truck. Once you are happy with the outline, go over the pencil sketch in fine black pen.

Step 4. You can now erase the pencil guidelines and bring the dumper truck to life by coloring it in!

Bus

Try your hand at this bus. Then have fun coloring it in with pens or pencils.

Top Tip!

Why not give your drawings a background, such as trees and houses? Start with basic shapes and gradually build up the detail.

Front-on View

Step 1. Sketch this simple guideline box for a front-on view of a bus.

Step 2. Inside the box, sketch in details such as a curved roof and large windshield.

Step 3. Add further details such as lights, then go over your sketch in black pen.

Step 4. Erase the guidelines and color in!

Side-on View

Step 1. Using a pencil and ruler, sketch a rectangle and two small circles.

Step 3. Build up the detail until you are happy with your sketch. Then carefully go over the pencil lines in black pen.

Step 2. Inside your guideline box, draw the outline of the bus, adding windows and doors.

Step 4. Finally, erase the pencil guidelines and color in your bus. You could add passengers, too!

Angled View

Step 1. First, draw a three-dimensional shape using slanting rectangles. Add two circles to show where the wheels will go.

Step 2. Next, sketch the outline of the bus inside your guideline box. Include doors and windows, and add wheel arches.

Step 3. Build up the detail and add markings. Once you are happy with your sketch, go over the pencil lines in black pen.

Step 4. Erase any remaining pencil lines, then choose a smart color scheme for your bus and color it in.

13

Truck

Put your drawing skills to the test by having a go at this powerful truck.

Fact File

Trucks have large, powerful engines, which they use to pull weights of more than 11 tons.

Side-on View

 1

 2

 3

Step 1. For a side-on view, use a ruler and pencil to sketch these guidelines.

Step 2. Next, draw the shape of the truck and guidelines for the side bars.

Step 3. Build up the details in pencil, adding lights, mirror, side bars and wheel hubs. Then go over your pencil lines in black pen.

Step 4. Erase any pencil lines and color in your truck. Why not add a smart company logo?

Front-on View

 1

Step 1. For your guidelines, draw four squares, as shown.

 2

Step 2. Next, draw the truck's outline inside your guideline boxes.

3

Step 3. Build up the details, then go over the pencil lines in black pen.

4

Step 4. Erase the pencil guidelines and color in your truck.

 4

Angled View

 1

Step 1. Using a pencil and ruler, sketch these guideline shapes. Try and copy the angles of the sloping lines shown here.

Step 2. You can now start to fill in the truck's outline shape. Notice the position of the wheel arches and front bumper.

 2

Step 4. Erase any remaining pencil lines and color in your truck. Include dark shadows around the side bars and tires.

 3

Step 3. Sketch in more details and then go over your pencil outline in black pen.

 4

Fire Truck

Look out! Here comes an exciting red fire truck to draw.

Fact File

As well as carrying hoses, a ladder and a water cannon, modern fire trucks may also have ramming pads to move obstructions out of the way.

Front-on View

Step 1. Sketch a set of guideline boxes using these shapes.

Step 2. Fill in the outline of the fire truck.

Step 3. Carefully add lots of detail, then go over your pencil lines in black pen.

Step 4. Color your truck bright red!

Side-on View

Step 1. First, sketch two guideline boxes, two circles for wheels, and a line for the ladder.

Step 2. Next, draw the outline of your truck and add details—ladder, lights, windows and wheel arches.

Step 3. Build up the details and draw in the central stripe. Then go over your pencil lines in black pen.

Step 4. Erase any remaining guidelines and color your truck in bright red, to make it easily recognizable.

Angled View

Step 1. To create a three-dimensional guideline box, sketch a slanting rectangle split into two, a slanting square and two circles for wheels.

Step 2. Next, draw the truck's outline and begin to add detail and definition. Include windows and, on top, a siren, a long light and the ladder.

Step 3. Build up more detail, then go over the pencil lines in black pen.

Step 4. Erase the guidelines and color in. Some trucks have a white or yellow stripe to make them stand out at night.

Cement Mixer

The trickiest bit of a cement mixer to draw is the cone-shaped mixer itself.

Fact File

A cement mixer keeps turning all the time to stop the cement inside it from going solid too soon.

Front-on View

Step 1. Sketch this guideline shape for your cement mixer.

Step 2. Draw the outline, using the top box for both the windshield and hood.

Step 3. Add lights, mirrors and radiator bars, then go over your pencil lines in pen.

Step 4. Color in your mighty mixer!

Side-on View

Step 1. Start by sketching three circles, then a square and two rectangles. These are the guideline shapes for your cement mixer.

Step 2. Next, outline the driver's cab and the mixer, which is roughly the shape of an ice-cream cone.

Step 3. Add details to the mixer, as shown here. Once you are happy with your drawing, go over the pencil lines in pen.

Step 4. Erase any remaining guidelines and color in your cement mixer with pens or pencils.

Angled View

Step 2. Next, copy the outline shown here into your guideline boxes. The three-dimensional wheels soon make the drawing take shape.

Step 1. Lightly sketch these basic shapes to represent the driver's cab, the mixer and the wheels. Notice that the wheels are ovals, not circles.

Step 3. Add further details until you are happy, then go over your pencil lines in black pen.

Step 4. Erase any remaining pencil guidelines and color in your mixer in bright, bold colors.

Monster Truck

Have fun drawing this monster racing truck!

Fact File

Bob Chandler was the first person to build a monster truck, in the 1970s. He named it Bigfoot!

Front-on View

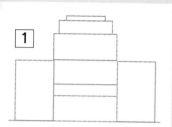

Step 1. Sketch eight rectangles to create the basic shape of the truck.

Step 2. Curve the edges of the body and wheels. Add suspension bars and lights.

Step 3. Draw the tire treads and other details, then go over in pen.

Step 4. Erase the guidelines and color in your monster truck.

Side-on View

Step 1. Sketch two large circles and a rectangle, then add two smaller rectangles on top.

Step 2. Draw the truck's outline inside the boxes.

Step 3. Add details to your monster truck, including tire treads, lights and windows. Then go over your outline in black pen.

Step 4. Erase any pencil guidelines and color in your mighty monster.

Angled View

Step 1. Start by lightly sketching three cylinders for the wheels and two boxes for the truck's body. Take your time to work out the angles.

Step 2. Draw the truck's curved outline inside the guide boxes. Then carefully erase the straight lines of the boxes. Pencil in lights, windows and suspension bars.

Step 3. Pencil in further details such as tire treads and any markings you may want to include. Once you are happy with the sketch, go over it in black pen.

Step 4. Finally, erase any remaining pencil lines, and color in and decorate your monster racer.

Airplane

Now that you've mastered land vehicles, try your hand at some fantastic airplanes!

Fact File

The Wright brothers built the first successful airplane and made the first controlled human flight on December 17th, 1903.

Side-on View

Step 1. First, sketch a long rectangle, two smaller rectangles to represent the wheels, another rectangle for the cockpit and a square for the plane's tail.

Step 2. Using your boxes as guidelines, draw a side-on view of the plane. Include its wheels, propeller, tail fin, cockpit and wings (on top of the cockpit).

Step 3. Add more details such as doors, handles and tail parts. Once you are happy with the drawing, go over it in black pen.

Step 4. Erase the guideline boxes and color in your plane using pens or pencils. Don't be afraid to highlight parts or add some markings.

Flying High!

Make your plane soar with these underneath and above views!

Top Tip!

Experiment with different paper and pencils to find favorites that work best for you.

Underneath View

Step 1. First, sketch two three-dimensional boxes for the plane's body. Then add the shapes shown here for the tail and wings.

Step 2. Next, carefully copy the outline of the plane into your guideline boxes.

Step 3. Continue adding details until you are happy with your picture. Then go over your pencil lines in black pen.

Step 4. Erase any remaining guidelines. Now bring your airplane to life by coloring it in. Have fun with the colors!

Above View

Step 1. Create your guideline boxes, as shown above. Try to get the angles right, and keep your lines straight with a ruler.

Step 2. Sketch the plane's curved outline inside the boxes, and begin to add details such as wheels, windows and propeller.

Step 3. Add wing supports, propeller blades and any other details. Then go over your pencil outline in black pen.

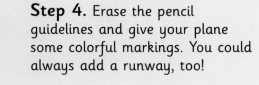

Step 4. Erase the pencil guidelines and give your plane some colorful markings. You could always add a runway, too!

Spitfire
The famous Spitfire is great to draw!

Fact File
The Spitfire was a British single-seater fighter plane used throughout World War Two.

Angled View

Step 1. Create your guideline boxes, as shown above.

Step 2. Draw the plane's outline, with its wide, curved wings.

Step 3. Add details and markings. Then go over your pencil lines in black pen.

Step 4. Erase the guidelines and have fun adding the Spitfire's distinctive colors.

Front-on View

Step 1. To create the Spitfire's basic shape, draw a rectangle with a circle inside and add lines to represent the wings and tail.

Step 2. Next, sketch the outline of the wings, body and tail around the guidelines, and add wheels.

Step 3. Add more detail, including a large circle around the body to suggest the propeller in motion. Then go over your pencil outline in black pen.

Step 4. Erase any remaining pencil lines and give your Spitfire its famous brown and dark green colors.

Side-on View

Step 1. Start by sketching a long rectangle, followed by three smaller rectangles.

Step 2. Draw the outline of the Spitfire inside the guideline boxes, and begin to add details such as wheels and a propeller.

Step 3. Continue to add detail, including the markings. Then go over your outline in black pen.

Step 4. Erase the guidelines and color in your Spitfire, giving it a green and brown camouflage pattern.

Flying Fortress

Are you brave enough to take on this mighty Flying Fortress?

Fact File

The Flying Fortress was a heavy bomber flown by the British and Americans in World War Two.

Angled View

Step 1. First, lightly sketch your guideline boxes by following the example above.

Step 2. Using the boxes as a guide, draw in the outline shape of the Flying Fortress.

Step 3. Add details such as the cockpit and propellers, and draw markings on the wings and body. Go over your outline in black pen.

Step 4. Erase the pencil guidelines and color in your mighty Flying Fortress.

Front-on View

Step 1. Start by sketching a rectangle for the body, two long lines for the wings, a short line for the tail and four small circles to show where the propellers go.

Step 2. Draw the shape of the plane's body inside the rectangle, and add wings and a tail around the guidelines.

Step 3. Next, pencil in the propellers and add detail to the body. Once you are happy with your picture, go over your pencil outline in fine black pen.

Step 4. Erase the pencil guidelines, color the Flying Fortress in gray and add its distinctive yellow markings.

Eurofighter Typhoon

The streamlined Eurofighter Typhoon is based on a triangle shape.

Fact File

The Eurofighter Typhoon has a very aerodynamic shape, meaning the air flows around it easily, allowing it to travel very fast through the sky.

Angled View

Step 1. Start by sketching a long box and mark its central line. Then add wing and tail shapes.

Step 2. Carefully copy the plane's body shape into your guideline box. Notice where to place the tip of the nose.

Step 3. Add more detail and then go over your pencil outline in black pen.

Step 4. Erase the pencil guidelines and color in your supersonic, super stealthy Eurofighter Typhoon.

Front-on View

Step 2. Sketch the plane's body shape inside the rectangle, and draw the wings and tail around the guidelines.

Step 1. Start by drawing a rectangle. Add lines for the wings and tail. Draw a small circle at the end of each wing, and another underneath each wing for the missiles.

Step 3. Continue to add detail, and then go over your pencil outline in black pen.

Step 4. Erase any pencil lines and color in your fearsome jet fighter in a mean gray!

Boeing 747

Fly away to a distant land in this fantastic Boeing 747!

Fact File

The Boeing 747 is sometimes referred to as a "Jumbo Jet" or "Queen of the Skies."

Front-on View

Step 1. For your guidelines you'll need a rectangle, five lines and four circles.

Step 2. Next, build up the shape of your large, heavy plane around the guidelines.

Step 3. Add details such as the window, nose cone and engines. Then go over your pencil lines in black pen.

Step 4. Erase any remaining guidelines and color in your fabulous Boeing 747 passenger plane.

Angled View

Step 1. Start by drawing a long box to represent the body. Half way along, add two wing shapes.

Step 2. Draw the outline of the body inside your guideline box. Then add the tail and engines.

Step 3. Build up the detail, adding flaps and windows. Now go over your outline in black pen.

Step 4. Finally, erase any remaining pencil lines and color in your plane. You could even create a colorful design for the tail fin!

Side-on View

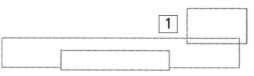

Step 1. Using a pencil and ruler, draw a long rectangle for the body, then two smaller ones to show the position of the wings and tail.

Step 2. Next, draw the outline of the plane inside your guideline boxes, following the example above.

Step 3. Add windows and the front part of the engines. Once you are happy with the picture, go over your outline in black pen.

Step 4. Erase the pencil guidelines and color in your Boeing 747. Don't forget to give it an eye-catching tail design!

Conclusion

The more you practice, the easier your drawing will become.

Now that you have drawn all the pictures in this book, why not have a go at doing some stunning drawings of your own?

Choose a vehicle and spend time looking at it before you begin. Try to see it in your mind as a series of basic shapes. Study its proportions and angles.

Perhaps the most important thing to remember is to always draw what you can actually see, not what you think something looks like!

Now take out your sketch pad, pencils, a sharpener, an eraser and a pen—**and get drawing!**

Drawing Cartoons

You can have great fun using your new drawing skills to create cartoon vehicles!

The technique you use is the same as when drawing "regular" cars, trucks and planes, except that now you can have fun changing the style and shape of the vehicle, and giving it cartoon features.

1

Step 1. Sketch a thin box for the lower part of the car's body, and two cylinders for wheels. For the fun top half of your cartoon car, sketch a tall box.

2

Step 2. Next, draw the car's outline. A very short hood makes the tall top half of the car look funnier.

3

Step 3. As well as distorting the car's shape, you can have fun changing its features. Large headlights look like eyes, and a small radiator looks like a nose! Work up the detail and go over your outline in pen.

4

Step 4. Finally, erase the pencil guidelines and color in your cheeky cartoon car.